To Future
Heartbreaks

Lia Harris

Published by Lee's Press and Publishing Company
www.LeesPress.net

This document is published by Lee's Press and Publishing Company located in the United States of America. It is protected by the United States Copyright Act, all applicable state laws and international copyright laws. The information in this document is accurate to the best of the ability of Lia Harris at the time of writing. The content of this document is subject to change without notice.

ISBN-13: **978-0999310366** *Paperback*
ISBN-10: **0999310364**

Table of Contents

4

To the hearts that have been broken ...

Deconstruction

If Only

If only I could go back in time, and change the past
So this pain that I'm feeling wouldn't last
If only I could revive myself
To not feel the way that I do
So I could be one of those free emotionless human
beings
If only I could discover a way,
I hope and pray this pain away,
To live life to the fullest,
If only I could be happy once again

My Soul Wrote This

My soul is trapped in the body of man, created by
man
where instead of having a frustration of using my
feet and hands
emotion and mental issues takeover
My soul feels drugged with over thinking,
With a hint of caring too much
My soul feels corrupted by the opinions of others
being let down by those I thought who wouldn't;
Feeling alone,
and worst of all depression.
My body might not be suffering, but my soul is;
Manipulated and abused, I don't think it can take
much more,
But every time I'm all alone, my soul cries
"freedom",
And dry tears run down my face
This isn't just me crying
It's my soul
I just feel its pain

I don't ever want to cry
Just because I have tried
And you didn't live up to the expectation

I don't ever want to try
Knowing that I'm wasting precious time
And you continue doing the same things

I don't want to waste time
because, true love is hard to find,
and I don't even believe it exists

I don't want true love
because it was never true,
and when I thought of true love
I was thinking of you

Let Them In

When you trap yourself in your own thoughts
It's hard to let someone else in

Tired of Stressing

I'm tired of stressing
From waiting on blessings

Why can't dreams come true?

I'm tired of stressing
From people not learning their lessons

Positivity; why can't I see through?

I'm tired of stressing,
Depression, I'm guessing?

Why does it leave me so blue?

I'm tired of stressing
All this pain in my chest, and

I think my heart has been bruised

Loneliness

Have you ever felt so lonely?
Where you have no one to talk to you,
No one to understand you
Some act like they understand,
and when they try to lend a helping hand it's not very
helpful,
If only people knew; loneliness is like the blues
The blues is the only route to choose
Even with a full house, I still feel lonely,
and I have thoughts that run through my head,
in which I wish it didn't.

Diamond in the Rough

I guess I am that diamond in the rough,
Made from the pressure of thoughts and people;
Man that's tough!
and just when I think I've had enough
It's too late; my heart has been cuffed by the pain
Which the pain drives me insane
It has me so confused
I'm in a different lane
Taking a path I've never been before

Now I'm lost; No I'm stuck
Because I'm still that diamond in the rough

But the real question is;
Am I hiding in the rough because I don't know my
own worth?
If so, is that the reason I still hurt?

You would think I am that diamond in the rough,
because people don't see my worth,
but I am keeping others from seeing it

Is that why I hurt?

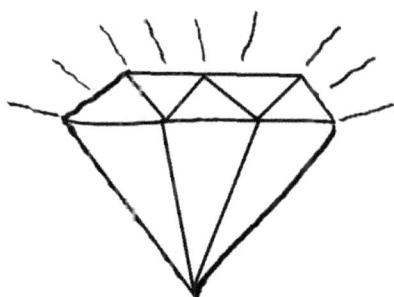

The Prettiest Flowers Even Wilt

It was standing straight up, as if it weren't bothered.
The bright red petals represent love.
The thorns represent the roses guard, and the
protection of its beauty.
Its beauty represents innocence
Although as beautiful as a rose can be, it can also be
deceptive.
Even though it stands up straight, you barely notice
the red petals are beginning to wilt. The roses red
petals aren't at its brightest, but the color is still
astounding to the eyes, but it no longer represents
love. The thorns no longer hold up its guard, and
begins to represent pain.
Although it's beautiful,
Don't be deceived of what happiness the rose can
bring.

Torn

Just as thin as paper
Fragile at heart
Treat it with delicacy
Or it will fall apart

All grown up
She's been through a lot
Has been put through so much
Forgave but never forgot

Failure, Pupils of deception,
Anything that hurts the heart

There are a lot of cruel things in this world
Please don't tarnish the heart
of what was once the little girl

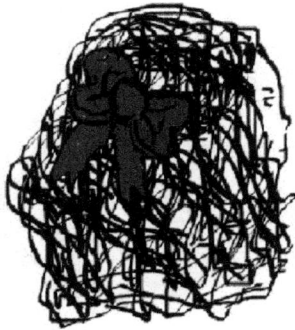

Such quietness can be so fearsome,
It can also be a killer
It could hold in so much pain,
And sometimes could be a loud cry for help

Dirty Laundry

If you keep getting someone to do your dirty laundry
You're only leaving a big stain on theirs,
That I don't think can be washed out or replaced
The love is still there
But I no longer want to suffer the pain.

Shades of Sadness

If there are fifty shades of grey, what shade am I?
I've been feeling blue...

Wanted

Is it truly what you desired?
Or something you still wanted around?
You can look into their eyes but not make a sound.

I have been kind to others,
But not to myself
I respect others,
But I haven't been respectful to myself
I care too much about others,
But I don't care too much about myself

Am I losing myself, for those who I don't want to
lose?

December 13th

"I love you"
Was the last thing that left his lips
Before he left out into the cold winter night
The warmth of his kiss on my forehead
will always be remembered

I am a book with one of those covers,
Where no one wants to open me up
They don't want to read or understand me;
Therefore I am judged

We live in our dreams so much that when we wake
up to reality,
It's nothing but a nightmare

People are so quick to show what's in the light,
But won't shine lights on the things done in the dark

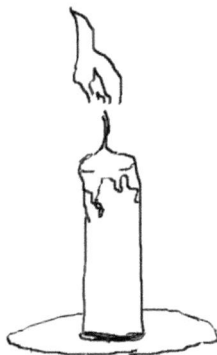

I guess I will always be that rare gem that people
find
Don't know the worth or value of it;
So they leave it behind

I walk around with my head bow low
I am constantly thinking on how my life will go
I don't want to interfere with the waves or the flows
To my understanding, this is how life is supposed to
go

People get mad over little things,
Turn around, roll their eyes, and begin to belittle
things
Instead of respecting others,
they only respect the lavish things,
and to my heart and soul,
oh what the pain it brings

Don't be deceived by the waterfalls,
They won't end in a "happily ever after" after all
Don't be naïve and go towards something so fast
Trust and believe that it will not last.

Boundaries

Why break the limits and the boundaries,
I think I found who you're bound to be
You don't care about my well-being
Crossing these boundaries should be a crime
You are way over the limit, and crossed the line
Do my heart a favor and don't waste my time
Don't waste my precious time

Stepping on Shards of Glass

Stepping on shards of glass as if doesn't hurt me.
But on my face the pain you will see
The pain is so numbing that I forget it even hurts
This makes the situation sound even worse

Stay True

I believed in you
To be as true as I thought you were
But you really fooled me,
It's like my mind threw me a curve

I couldn't catch it, I wasn't expecting it
Trying hard to connect the puzzle,
But the pieces wouldn't fit

I've now given up on you,
because you didn't stay true

Human Trash Can

Having problems dumped on me,
Like I'm supposed to always solve them
But when I put my problems out there,
They get ignored
That's a problem

When I bring up something new,
Problems are dug up from their past,
And dumped on me,
As if I were to pick up their trash

Needed

She said she was leaving,
And never coming back
With a straight face,
He was slowly having a panic attack
He asked her to stay,
He begged and pleaded
Then she realized that she was the one he needed

Lonely Nights

The worsts thing than being lonely
Is being lonely at night
It's not the darkness or the creepy sounds that give
fright
It's the mind, when it begins to wonder
Making me think about certain things,
Then I begin to ponder
The mind can be a frightening thing
Especially with all the hurt and confusion it brings

Hanging on for dear life,
Sometimes I feel like as if my grip is too tight,
So tight I begin to lose grip
"I can't hold on anymore"
Leaves my cold lips

Future

Blinded by this person for many years,
Every time the small talk became a silence,
It brought me to tears
The small talk always brought me to fear
But I was always taught to focus on me and my
future career
Now it's close to the future,
And I don't know what to do
I feel like all my future would be missing is you

Used and Abused

In this heart of mine,
I were close to you,
But our friendship is something that was abused,
Like learning something new,
I was confused
That I was someone that was just being used

All I wanted was for you to stay,
I never noticed I pushed everyone away,
This wasn't a game that was being played
It was just my way of saying I was feeling like
I was living in the worse of my days

Abyss

I have fallen into the abyss of melancholy
Where I was lonely in the dark
People said they screamed my name,
But I didn't hear them at all
I was deprived of sleep,
And stripped of my warmth
With no one by my side to hold
I sat alone desperately
Thinking of ways not to be so cold

Something's Missing

Looking for something, that I've been missing
Nothing seemed to fit the description
People tried to tell me different
But they would never know
because they didn't listen
There is not enough time
Time is ticking
My life needs a little fixing
Before it's too late

You were gone with the wind
That blew within the leaves of the trees
Even though you're gone
I hope you still remember me
Even though you're gone,
I hope and pray
That the memories we once shared
Won't fade away

My mind is a maze
I've been wondering around in it for days
Trying to think of ways
To stop thinking of things that ruin my happiest
days,
but mind games;
This maze likes to play

One day I will outsmart this maze

Grapevine

Are those really grapes on the grape vine?
Only produced to make a fine wine
To make it look like one good kind
But what came out was a waste of time

Those things on the vine weren't grapes ,
They were taken away and replaced
To make everything artificially a disgrace,
And when others put it to their lips to distinguish its
taste ,
They think the one who planted the grapevine wears
a cape

You can't always trust the grapes on the grapevine
because the person's name that was planted on it
Could be the complete opposite
With a heart that's pure and kind

Just like the stars in the sky I enjoyed watching you
shine,
every time you took one step forward,
I was right behind
even when I was present
I don't think you noticed,
your light begin to dim and change
before I could help you shine again,
you lead me down the wrong way
then it was too late

Boomerang

Just when you think you threw it out of existence,
it always returns
Why when we let go of something,
it always comes back?
No matter how many times we screw bolts, and
tighten chains,
For it to stay away

It always comes back like a boomerang

Hurting

Why am I hurting?
Was it really worth it?
All of the pain

Why am I hurting?
You know I don't deserve it
all of the pain
drives me insane
all of the memories made
are dead,
and gone..

Psychotic

How can a heart that's so pure
be misconfigured and ruined by life?
Others tormenting, and nagging with the mind
making you and what you say worthless
and you don't know whether it's the time
to smile,
I haven't did that in a while ,
your mind is stuck in a very cold place
the thought just keeps rolling through the dark
forest in your mind
and you begin to think if it is that time
before you begin to think you're psychotic

Even though we come from two different places,
With different journeys and paths,
I hope I can make it
Living with a tragedy that only made me,
Living in my negative thoughts
like at a luxurious hotel with a grade C
when I am surrounded by nothing but blessings
I'm too closed-minded ,
so I continue to keep stressing

Always trying to get it together
here lately I've been through some stormy weather
When lightning strikes,
here comes the thunder
it struck me so hard,
my mind starts to wonder
As the sky gets darker, it begins to rain
Who knew that it could cause so much pain
It begins to get cold, as the temperature changes
My life is a storm it drives me insane
The storm cloud fills the night sky
Tornadoes and hurricanes make it a bumpy ride
I'm always here waiting on the next day
So I can be happy sliding down the sun's rays
My whole life I've been hearing about this eternity
of sunshine
I want to seek this happiness, and leave the storm
behind
Without the storms clouds, I would have some
clarity
Rain and dark clouds makes it hard to see
Sunshine is to lead the way
And to release me from my stormy days

As time passes by
It only reminds me of
where I am now
and where I should be

I'm living in a world full of destruction
with a lot of people who cause obstruction
where someone could mentally and physically take
you abduction
when it's supposed to be all about construction.

Reconstruction

Like once a broken vase,
my heart began to mend its tiny millions of pieces
back together again

I want to be the bird that's free
I want to be the butterfly that flaps its wings
I want to be the humming bird that always sings

Natural things like this
Has always been beautiful to me

I want to be the clouds the freely flow through the
sky
I want to be the autumn leaves that fall gently from
the trees at night
I want to be the shining stars by the moonlight

Calm, gentle and free
I wouldn't mind if that were me

As I walk upon the trail of faith
I forget how many steps I had to take
To get to where I am now
I just begin to think of where I would
have been if I would of walked off that
trail,
Maybe lost hopes and dreams

Disappear, Reappear

How is it that something's disappear, and then
reappear?
Like that toy you lost as a kid, and then as it
reappears, your childhood has once returned;
or like that memory that once disappeared,
but an instant flashback brings back that moment
Things that you once thought they would be gone
forever,
But return back into your presence;
Physically, mentally, and emotionally
There is no magic to the disappearing and
reappearing
of things, but it could be that it's meant to be back in
your life

but who knows?
It could be a lesson or a blessing,
or even a miracle
Just don't let it be a nightmare.

My happiness can't depend on anyone else; at the end of the day I got myself.
Friends are temporary, family is forever, and the man upstairs can get me through any type of weather.
I am the only one that can determine my happiness, I am the only one that can feel the bliss, its up to me to take the direction of positivity,
and to believe in such a light that can brighten the darkness of a tunnel, my day, and the smile that's brought upon my face
Happiness isn't something that's given, it's something you make of life in any situation, and if everyone could see this through happiness will be swept through every nation,
But we are afraid.
Afraid of being too happy as if it were an epidemic, that will soon cause us pain
Little do we know, we think pain which deprives us of our happiness, and we control our emotions, and the way we feel
Happiness is the key to all that heals

Let the light feel in the cracks of my shattered heart
To where it doesn't feel like I'm falling apart
Let the light show and guide me towards the right
path
To where it's everlasting and will always last
I want that little light to shine
Shine as bright as ever, as if it were mine
I want to be that light, which shines its best
Through the bad times like, depression, and even
stress

I am that light that will lead the way
To better living, and happier days

Secrets

Why hide?
The generation we live in there is no surprise
If you keep it in, you'll blind people's eyes
with one truth, and a million lies

Failing

No one ever said life was easy
It comes with obstacles, hardships, and troubles
just because you don't get it the first time
don't let it burst your bubble
It may be a mountain,
and you won't succeed the first time
keep on trying, in the end
it will be worth the climb

Childish

Let me be free to think as a child
wear mitch-matching socks,
walk around with my hair wild

watching 90's cartoons,
chasing the ice cream trucks,
asking parents for dimes and nickels
to come up with a buck

And please don't tell me to "grow up",
those words are like a dose of medicine
that drips from adults lips
to cure the happiness of a child

The "Good" in Goodbye

There will always be greatness of "good"
Although "bye" can put an end to a lot of things
Find the "good" in it, and you'll be free
Of all the sorrows, that follows behind it tomorrow

Fire

Burning rages through the heart
You begin to get furious
Anger may takeover
But don't let it make you delirious.

I run like the water in the sink,
not knowing my next destination,
or what river I will end up in

Masterpiece

Different from others,
To where you stand out
Everyone was made to be accepted as themselves
With every flaw, and every characteristic
Loving who you are, inside and out
Being a masterpiece is what it's about

She grew from the garden, not knowing
what she could blossom into

Believe (Speak It Into Existence)

I believe I have a dream
I believe I can achieve it
I know I can achieve it, if I believe in it

Butterfly

You'll always have to let go of something you love
Just like a butterfly when it leaves its cocoon
At one point it needed it, its warmth and love,
But once it sees it doesn't need it anymore
it leaves and flies away freely,
leaving the cocoon behind

As I look through the eye glass
I see things more clearly,
I wasn't blind before
It's just my perception of everything changed

Who Am I? (Not My Looks)

Fair skin during the winter
Sun kissed during the summer
I am who I am
I'm like no other
I have my beliefs
I will remain the same
It's not about my looks
My identity is my name

The Wise Owl

One day you will get as wise as the owls in the trees
Your eyes will be wider, and you'll see what you did
to me
The things that you did, broke me down but made
me strong
But as you transform into that owl, you'll know you
had a good one all along

Skin and Bones

Growing up,
I've always been told I look like skin and bones
but underneath all the flesh we look the same
and that's one thing you cannot change

Keep in mind the people, who now hate you,
Because of a toxic relationship,
once had love for you
They adored you,
and found happiness in you at one point

Open & Closed Doors

There are so many doors open,
But a few that are closed
Temptation leads us to the closed ones
While the open ones lead us down a road

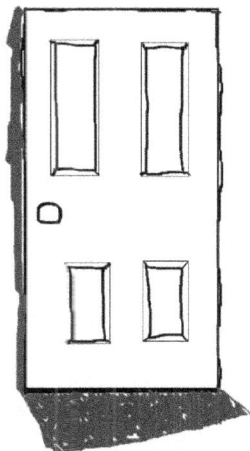

Set Me Free

Set me free
like a feather of a bird that falls from the nest of a
tree
Set me free
like the pollen of a flower that's carried by the bees
Set me free
by the warmth,
and the feeling of home of your body,
as you welcome me into your arms

Fantasy

Life may not be a fantasy
It tends to be what you make it to be
This life may be a reality
But if you make your own magic
It could turn into the happiness you once dreamed

One day you will be tired of contemplating
over situations that won't matter

One day you will learn how to clean up the mess
After your heart has been shattered

One day you will know that people
act the way they do for attention and show

One day you will get it together
Evolve, prosper and grow

One day you will be able to realize who's real,
and pick out the frauds

One day you will make it,
because the grace of God

There can't be fireworks
without that spark

No Fools Here

Honey,
Don't ever feel like you're being played for a fool,
because the fool is the one playing you

My Decision

Was my decision what I had envisioned?
It's like my heart, mind and soul
don't work together,
it causes collision
my minds on a mission, soul thinking religion,
and my heart is somewhere it has no business

Was my decision right?
has it opened up closed doors,
or at least shined a light,
so bright that I can seek towards a dream
of mine down a path on a dark night
was it strong enough or was it even meant for me to
fight?

Was my decision a lousy choice?
Chosen by someone else because I have no voice?

My decision is my decision at the end of the day,
but as long as I have faith, God will lead the way.

Disappointment

It may destroy you mentally,
and sometimes it can creep around without you
knowing
although it may let you down
know it's not the fault of you
to cure this emotional feeling
you can start by mentally healing
to eliminating the thought or epistemic of
expectation

Tree of Life

Never forget the roots you have stemmed from,
You will always be connected with them
Whether you branch out
or simply just fall off

Promises (The Vow)

From using your pinky as a kid
to vowing as an adult
you always say you'll never break it,

From gazing into each other's eyes as if they mean it
If you're not going to live up to it
don't take it

Constructed

The Blooming of the Flower

Life is like a blooming flower
given birth by a single seed, shed by its mother
as it is planted into the womb of the ground,
it becomes a part of Mother Nature
it begins to grow as a single sprout
Where it is nurtured by the sun's rays,
And the April showers
Then as May approaches it becomes
a beautiful blooming flower,
Like the one that had given it life
In everything in life, it comes to the end
of its season,
but don't worry there will always be a reminder
of what was once the blooming flower

Change

Change,
I wish that I could explain,
Sometimes it can lead to a panic of the brain
it's just like a car when it switches lanes
Sometimes it can mess you up,
I can't stand change

Change,
It could be something new,
why does it show up out of nowhere
out of the blue
this change is nothing that you can pick or choose

Change,
it's forever to stay
if you try to change, change
There is just no way

Change,
sometimes I wish you could leave,
sometimes change can be the best thing to receive

I reeled them in with the best bait there was;
honesty, trust, consistency,
and love

My happiness you can't take it,
My heart you can't break it
My eyes, they are unclouded from the negativity

Positivity,
Overtakes all the rain
This resembles the pain
That overtakes my sunshine

Sunshine,
I want an eternity of,
And I'll find it as long as I have the man above
even though life comes to push and shove
I shout "no more"!
No more!

Independent

It's not about being lonely
it's about having your own
where you can have a crown
and rule over your own throne

Home

Home,
Where the heart is
Where the mind is comfortable to think
Where you feel warm
Where you feel welcome
Where there can be trust
Where there is love
Where there is God.

If it's a secret
you can keep it
but you can't keep me

No Makeup

The moon doesn't need the stars
It stands out on its own
Without the stars it is still beautiful

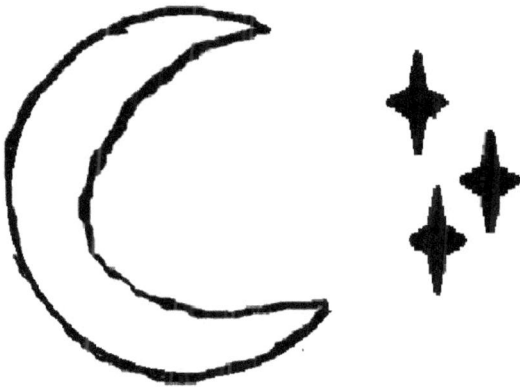

For once she felt warm,
And it was without the sun

Angel

Posture so heavenly
Fierce in the heart
Mind so strong
Where do I start?
Beautiful in and out
Soul so golden
Bright like a star
An angel is what you are

The world is yours
Let the cloud be your pillow
and the sun's warmth, your blanket

I would always wonder, what it would take to be
beautiful
until I saw, I always was beautiful on the inside
that the outside never really mattered
and eventually the inside,
effected what I had on the outside.

Strong

Growing up is hard to do
When all people do is pick at you
They pick at your flaws
Hoping that soon you'll fall

They always don't want you to proceed
You begin to lack confidence then don't succeed
You work so hard that you scrape your knees
Continue fighting as you still bleed

Of your dreams you are the beholder
You brush everything off, and lift the weight off
your shoulders
And still carrying rocks, and pushing boulders
And continue to fight like a soldier

There is beauty in simplicity,
Like the tides of the ocean and the rising of the sun,
The simple things in life can be just as beautiful

Pick up every piece of your heart, and mend it into
something more beautiful than before

The Steps I Take

I never knew how far I could go until I took my first
step,
Now I am walking with my head held high,
And confident within every step I take

The Sun & Stars

The warmth of the sun touching my skin feels like a
million warm kisses
The million stars that grasp the sky, begin to make
me think about the million wishes

Enlightenment

I am hiding behind the shadows of misery
my heart deformed by the tragic history
of everything that broke my heart,
as a person it made me fall apart
with all the pain I turned it into art
to release the troubles and the struggles,
that I hide beneath
to tell the stories of how I got back on my feet
through the battles, that ended up in defeat
and through the dark shadows,
the enlightenment I seek

I Write Because I Love It

Just with pen and paper I enter into a whole other
world
As my fingertips express what's on my mind,
and the ink establishes who I am,
and what I've been through

Paradise

I just want to live in paradise,
it doesn't have to include the expensive things
and everything nice, or a price,
it's where I achieve my dreams and live a nice life,
where I don't have to worry or think twice

The Ride of Life

Everyone experiences the thrilling ride of life
It has its downs and ups,
and sometimes might turn you upside down
to where you either make the best of the ride,
or get nauseous and sick from it
if you continue the riding of life
after all it has put you through,
you have conquered life itself,
and continue riding it with no fear

Unity

It is amazing how people come together as one,
Nothing is more beautiful as the construction
of what one unity could do together

It is Time to Break the Wall and Live

She built her walls up without knowing what's on
the other side,
when she finally knocked it down she found herself,
and another world of adventure

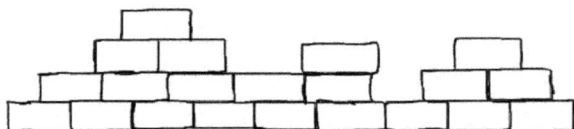

Some Still Care

Without a doubt
They cared
About your success
Your future
Your life,
Your happiness
It wasn't about the words they expressed
To show they cared
But the actions they took to
Express how they felt
That's how you know someone is real.

Yourself

When you wake up
and see yourself in the mirror
and you don't see yourself,
You see someone else
someone more bright,
someone who looks like they
have bloomed,
someone who
fought their own battles,
and survived, and ready to share
their testimony
about their trials and tribulations
you have already found the person
that's been looking you in the face every day,
knowing what you are capable of

The Wind and Leaves

As I dance in the autumn leaves,
I notice how the wind sings in my ear encouraging
me
to not have a care in the world,
because, I am just as bright,
and beautiful as the colorful leaves that fall,
and raise me up as I continue to dance,
and as the wind continues to sing

Brotherhood, Sisterhood

Nothing is better than when your brothers
and sisters are on your side
and when they lift each other up
when another has fallen

Construction of the Heart

The construction of my own heart
Brought tears to my eyes,
But they were tears of joy
Knowing that my heart was whole again

Let the healing begin ...

About the Book

From disappointments, death, failures, betrayal, having to grow up, change, decisions, negativity, stress, love, toxic relationships, friendships, family, *To future heartbreaks* is a collection of poems that comes from that broken heart, but from that broken heart, can become a world of happiness depending on how you would build yourself back up from the heartbreaks and pain, and just remember something broken can be fixed better yet, it can become something better than it was before.

About the Author

Lia Harris is a young upcoming author, who enjoys the world of poetry, and uses it as an outlook to inspire others, and hopes to continue inspiring others
by just picking up a pen and paper and letting people into the world of what her and others have been through. She found her inspiration through the good and the bad, through certain trials and tribulations, and molded it into literature and art, thriving to one day help someone who might need the inspiration.